Deliver Us

Church Times Study Guides

Deliver Us: Exploring the Problem of Evil
Mike Higton

Doing What Comes Naturally? The Christian Tradition and Sexual Ethics
Neil Messer

Embracing the Day: Exploring Daily Prayer
Stephen Burns

Faith Under Fire: Exploring 1 Peter and Revelation
John Holdsworth

The Fellowship of the Three: Exploring the Trinity
Jane Williams

Here is the News!
John Holdsworth

Immersed in Grace: Exploring the Baptism
Stephen Burns

Living the Thanksgiving: Exploring the Eucharist
Stephen Burns

The Mighty Tortoise: Exploring the Church
Jane Williams

Prophets and Loss: Exploring the Old Testament
John Holdsworth

The Same But Different: The Synoptic Gospels
John Holdsworth

Who Do You Say that I Am? Exploring Our Images of Jesus
Jane Williams

Yours Sincerely: Exploring the Letters of the New Testament
John Holdsworth

Church Times Study Guide

Deliver Us

Exploring the Problem of Evil

Mike Higton

CANTERBURY PRESS
Norwich

© Mike Higton 2007

First published in 2007 by the Canterbury Press Norwich
(a publishing imprint of Hymns Ancient & Modern Limited,
a registered charity)
9–17 St Alban's Place, London N1 0NX

www.scm-canterburypress.co.uk

All rights reserved. No part of this publication may be
reproduced, stored in a retrieval system, or transmitted,
in any form or by any means, electronic, mechanical,
photocopying or otherwise, without the prior permission of
the publisher, Canterbury Press

British Library Cataloguing in Publication data

A catalogue record for this book is available
from the British Library

ISBN 978-1-85311-785-5
5-pack ISBN 978-1-85311-786-2

Typeset by Regent Typesetting, London
Printed and bound by Gallpen Colour Print, Norwich

Contents

Leaders' Notes — vii
Introduction — xi

1 What's the Problem? — 1
2 The Standard Conversation — 5
3 Changing the Subject — 11
4 A Different Approach — 21
5 Conclusion — 29

References and Further Reading — 31

Leaders' Notes

Planning sessions

Remember

Keep in mind the ethos: 'The course is an attempt to share, not to talk down.'

There is enough material and exercises to offer a choice if you are having a single session: familiarize yourself with all material and select.

Prioritize

Choose the most important aims for your group. Deciding which aims to focus on will help you select the most appropriate material and exercises.

Decide the balance, in your local context, between learning aims relating to the course content and other needs (e.g. enabling people to meet socially, encouraging people to speak about faith). This also helps selecting appropriate material and process.

Planning

Have a variety of different ways of working – e.g. discussion in twos or threes, discussion all together in plenary, one person talking, personal reflection, opportunities to write down, etc. Changing the pace aids concentration. Also people have different learning styles, and sessions are likely to work best if they include elements that cater to the variety of ways in which people learn.

Plan how the group will work through your chosen exercises. There are many ways of using the material.

When introducing new concepts or material, think whether there is any additional background information that might help people without much prior knowledge.

Decide what prayer/worship opportunities to include. Some may find it practical to have optional worship beforehand: others might want something that contrasts with the 'wordiness' of discussion.

Let participants know if they need to bring anything with them, or if you want them to do anything before the session.

Getting started

Sitting comfortably

A circle rather than rows encourages discussion/participation. Arrange seating so all can see each other's faces.

Forming the group

Make sure everybody knows who everyone is, and introduce the purpose of the session. Explain how it will be shaped and the time when it will end (make sure you finish then!). Using a quick introductory exercise can give each person an opportunity to give his or her name and say something. Give limits for contributions (e.g. 'one sentence'); otherwise they tend to get longer going round the circle.

Ground-rules/Boundaries/Group covenants

It helps if all are clear and agreed on how the group will run at the beginning. You may want to suggest a few 'ground rules' (e.g. not interrupting/confidentiality) and give the group a chance to suggest others.

Group facilitation

The leader/facilitator needs to attend to the dynamics and smooth working of the group, as well as the course material. Maintaining the group needs skills of encouragement and 'gate-keeping' to help people get involved and keep communication channels open.

Affirm contributions. If someone is criticized (by you or anyone else – and however well you know they can take it) it can discourage others, who may avoid comments or questions that might be risky.

Remind the whole group about the agreed ground-rules if and when necessary.

Concerns about those who participate too much or too little can often be helped by changing the process and giving people a task in smaller groups. The shy get an opportunity to speak and the over-vociferous can't dominate the whole group.

When you subdivide during a session, always have at least three sub-groups in a room. If there are two groups they listen to each other and get distracted.

Ensure people know they can raise questions and how to do it appropriately. Question time can operate in different ways, e.g.:

(a) Have a 'questions board' where people can put up questions (possibly written on 'post-it' notes) as they occur to them. Have time planned to address these.
(b) Gather in small discussion groups to raise questions – some people feel more confident voicing queries in a small group. Others in the group may respond to some, and the group can select a key question to contribute to a plenary.

Introduction

When I was growing up, there was a children's television programme called *Why Don't You?* The opening titles asked the question, 'Why don't you just switch off your television set and go and do something less boring instead?' before giving way to a magazine-style programme full of ideas for things you *could* have been doing if you weren't watching it. This booklet, though its content hardly resembles that of *Why Don't You?*, serves a similarly paradoxical purpose, because my hope is to convince you that responding to the problem of evil is not something that can be done by booklets, by ideas or by arguments – but only by lives lived in a certain way. The booklet would perhaps have been better titled: 'Responding to evil: Why don't you just put this booklet down and go and do something more useful instead?' But you'll have to read on in order to know why I think that's good advice.

1

What's the Problem?

Most students of theology in the first half of the nineteenth century would at some point have found themselves with William Paley's 1802 *Natural Theology* in their hands, reading an account of how the natural world in all its parts demonstrated the existence of a benevolent God:

> In every nature, and in every portion of nature, which we can descry, we find attention bestowed upon even the minutest parts. The hinges in the wings of an *earwig*, and the joints of its antennae, are as highly wrought, as if the Creator had nothing else to finish. We see no signs of diminution of care by multiplicity of objects, or of distraction of thought by variety. We have no reason to fear, therefore, our being forgotten, or overlooked, or neglected. (p. 376)

This marvellous world, so carefully and lovingly designed and built, does admittedly contain some suffering – some 'privation' and 'disappointment' – but if we see this from a religious perspective we will admit that even these are well-designed contrivances, 'not without the most salutary tendencies' (p. 372), and that

> Health and sickness, enjoyment and suffering, riches and poverty, knowledge and ignorance, power and subjection, liberty and bondage, civilisation and barbarity, have all their offices and duties, all serve for the *formation* of character. (p. 367)

After all,

> Of all views under which human life has ever been considered, the most reasonable, in my judgment, is that which regards it as a state

of *probation* ... It is not a state of unmixed happiness, or of happiness simply; it is not a state of designed misery, or of misery simply; it is not a state of retribution; it is not a state of punishment ... It accords much better with the idea of its being a condition calculated for the production, exercise, and improvement of moral qualities. (p. 366)

The world was, according to Paley, the work of a creator whose intentions were transparently good, and whose power and ability were unlimited; and none of the vicissitudes of life or nature did anything but confirm his existence, power and benevolence.

It is perhaps an understatement to say that not everyone has been convinced by visions like Paley's, and specifically by the ease with which visions like his take human suffering and the suffering of the natural world to be fitting pieces of a beautiful jigsaw. One representative of the dissatisfaction felt by many was a nineteenth-century gentleman who had read and enjoyed Paley's books while a theology student at university. He was a keen amateur naturalist, and instead of heading from his theological studies into a position in the Church, as he and his family had intended, he found himself embarking on an impromptu career as an explorer, geologist, botanist and zoologist. Yet, fascinated and delighted though he was by the variety and intricacy of the natural world, he found that the more he saw of it the more it appeared to him as a world of 'cruelty ... incalculable waste ... death, famine, rapine'.[1] The number of species that had gone their way to extinction, the fierce and bloody competition of those that survived, the ever-presence of predators and parasites – how could these be the elements of a well-ordered and harmonious whole? The poet Tennyson was to put some of these same doubts into words in 1850. We have, he said, trusted

> ... that somehow good
> Will be the final goal of ill ...
> That nothing walks with aimless feet;

we have trusted that

> ... God was love indeed
> And love Creation's final law,
> Tho' *Nature, red in tooth and claw*
> With ravine, shriek'd against [t]his creed.
>
> *In Memoriam*, LIII, LV (emphasis mine)

All this, however, was not what finally caused our theology student turned naturalist to break decisively with Paley's creed. After all, in the same notes in which he wrote about the cruelty and incalculable waste of nature, he could still argue that 'from ... the concealed war of nature ... the highest good which we can conceive, the creation of the higher animals, has directly come'. That so much waste and loss has eventually produced such creatures as ourselves should, he said, 'exalt our notion of the power of the omniscient Creator'.[2]

No, the decisive blow against Paley's vision fell some years later, in 1851, when after a short but distressing illness, and even more distressing attempts at treatment, the naturalist's ten-year-old daughter died at a sanatorium in Malvern. Her name was Annie. It was a very ordinary tragedy and the ripples of loss and grief spread no further than they normally do, and eventually dissipated as they normally do, leaving lasting pain only for her family. But for her father the event crushed what remained of his Christian faith. The death of his beloved daughter finally made real and personal for him the blank, impartial cruelty of nature that his botanical and zoological researches had uncovered.[3] What finally made a benevolent deity impossible for him to believe in was not some overview of suffering's quantity, pervasiveness or persistence in the natural world, nor his glimpses of similar suffering in humanity at large, but a close-up of one dying child who for him was of inestimable value. The man's name was Charles Darwin, and the reasons for his loss of faith – both his general acknowledgement of the preponderance of suffering in the world at large, and the personal loss that drove that acknowledgement into his heart – are what we call 'the problem of evil'.

Looking back, always the spirit of joyousness rises before me as her emblem and characteristic: she seemed formed to live a life of happiness ... We have lost the joy of the household, and the solace of our old age:– she must have known how we loved her; oh that she could know how deeply, how tenderly we do still and shall ever love her dear joyous face.

Charles Darwin, 'The death of Anne Elizabeth Darwin'[4]

Exercise

Has your faith or that of anyone you know been undermined or overthrown by suffering?

Notes

1 Darwin, 1909, pp. 51–2.
2 Darwin, 1909, p. 52.
3 Adrian Desmond and James Moore, *Darwin*, London: Michael Joseph, 1991, p. 387. See also Randal Keynes, *Annie's Box: Charles Darwin, His Daughter, and Human Evolution*, London: Fourth Estate, 2001. A dramatization of Darwin's reaction can be found in a novel by Harry Thompson, *This Thing of Darkness*, London: Review, 2005, p. 529.
4 This is Darwin's own brief memorial to his daughter, written a week after her death. It can be found in *The Correspondence of Charles Darwin*, vol. 5, ed. Frederick Burkhardt, Cambridge: Cambridge University Press, 1990, Appendix II, pp. 540–2; this extract is from p. 542.

2

The Standard Conversation

When theologians and philosophers of religion refer to 'the problem of evil' they often have in mind not the challenge to faith that erupts from direct involvement in suffering, but the intellectual difficulty posed by the bare fact of suffering's widespread existence. How is it possible to sustain belief in a good God, they ask, when we can all see in front of us a world marred by pervasive and persistent suffering? This is the kind of problem that did not trouble Paley, and that Darwin at first found himself able to overcome; it found its most famous formulation in the work of the Scottish philosopher David Hume:

> Is [God] willing to prevent evil, but not able? then is he impotent. Is he able, but not willing? then is he malevolent. Is he both able and willing? whence then is evil?[1]

More recently, the argument has been spelt out somewhat differently. It has been said that the following four claims are incompatible:

1. Evil exists.
2. God is good.
3. God is omnipotent.
4. A good being will always eliminate evil as far as it is able.[2]

> ### Exercise
> Do you see the force of this argument against the existence of a good and all-powerful God?

> Can you think of any responses to it?
> Do you think it captures Darwin's eventual reason for losing his faith?

The philosophers and theologians who discuss this problem often distinguish between two kinds of evil: moral and natural. For instance, the *Internet Encyclopedia of Philosophy*, in one of its articles on the problem of evil, provides the following definitions:

> *Moral evil.* This is evil that results from the misuse of free will on the part of some moral agent in such a way that the agent thereby becomes morally blameworthy for the resultant evil. Moral evil therefore includes specific acts of intentional wrongdoing such as lying and murdering, as well as defects in character such as dishonesty and greed.
> *Natural evil.* In contrast to moral evil, natural evil is evil that results from the operation of natural processes, in which case no human being can be held morally accountable for the resultant evil. Classic examples of natural evil are natural disasters such as cyclones and earthquakes that result in enormous suffering and loss of life, illnesses such as leukaemia and Alzheimer's, and disabilities such as blindness and deafness (Trakakis).

The example most frequently cited when discussing *moral* evil – an example that is used to show up the glibness or inadequacy of at least some attempts to provide a resolution to the problem of evil – is the Holocaust: the calculated debasement, torture and murder of six million Jews, millions of Poles and Serbs, half a million Bosnians, hundreds of thousands of Roma, people with disabilities, tens of thousands of homosexual men, and many thousands more, by the Nazi regime in Germany.

For *natural* evil, there is no single example that provides the same intensity of focus, but older discussions often cite the 1755 Lisbon earthquake, which killed between 60,000 and 100,000 people and shook the confidence of Enlightenment Europe, and more recent discussions often cite the 2004 Indian Ocean tsunami, in which a quarter of a million people died.

> Come, ye philosophers, who cry, 'All's well',
> And contemplate this ruin of a world.
> Behold these shreds and cinders of your race,
> This child and mother heaped in common wreck,
> These scattered limbs beneath the marble shafts —
> A hundred thousand whom the earth devours,
> Who, torn and bloody, palpitating yet,
> Entombed beneath their hospitable roofs,
> In racking torment end their stricken lives.
> To those expiring murmurs of distress,
> To that appalling spectacle of woe,
> Will ye reply: 'You do but illustrate
> The iron laws that chain the will of God'?
>
> Voltaire, 'Poem on the Lisbon Disaster – or, an examination of the axiom, "All is well"', *Toleration and Other Essays*

'Theodicy' is the name given to the attempts made by theologians and philosophers of religion to justify continued belief in a good God despite the existence of such moral and natural evil. More bluntly translated, theodicy is the 'justification of God' – the attempt to argue that God deserves to be called good despite all the evil that exists in God's world.

Over the years there has been no shortage of attempts to provide a theodicy, and these arguments come in many flavours. The most prevalent theodicies, however, tend to have the same basic structure: they claim, as did Paley, that there is some greater good that God could only achieve by creating a world in which moral and natural evil is possible or unavoidable. The evil is there, and it is genuinely evil in itself, but (so the argument goes) it is there *for a reason*, and if and when that reason is fully known, we will accept that God was *justified* in allowing it. We will accept that evil's existence and prevalence is consistent with God's perfect goodness.

There are two versions of this kind of 'greater good' argument that are by far the most prevalent. The first is the 'free will' defence, which says that the greater good that God desires is the existence of beings capable of free response to God and to one another in love. This freedom that God desires for us, however, is precisely the same freedom that allows us to *refuse* love, and to turn to various forms of hatred and harm. God could not have preserved us from all such harm, so the argument goes, without depriving us of freedom, and depriving creation of its good goal.

The second defence, which sometimes goes by the name 'soul-making' theodicy, is related. It argues (in a similar vein to Paley) that personal suffering is a necessary part of the process by which we learn to become fully moral persons. The argument is not now that by making us the kind of beings capable of free response, God has also made suffering possible, but the other way around: God has permitted us to suffer, because it is the endurance of such suffering that allows us to become beings capable of free and loving response to one another and to God. This world is a 'vale of soul-making' – a place of preparation for a future with God.[3]

There are also two further versions of this kind of 'greater good' argument that, though rather less common now than the free-will and soul-making defences, have been prominent at other times. On the one hand there is what one might call the 'aesthetic defence', which says that God's desire is for us to recognize and delight in what is good, but that such recognition and delight is only possible if we have something with which to contrast the good: only if can compare the good with, and prefer it to, suffering and evil can we truly delight in it.

An example of the 'aesthetic' defence can be found in Jill Paton Walsh's novel, *Knowledge of Angels*, when the monk Beneditx takes the sceptic Palinor to see a mosaic portraying the beauty of heaven. 'Do you see that even to make such a scene of brightness as this, the master artificer needed tessarae of dark glass as well as of bright glass? ... dullness is in the service of light here; dark pieces are in the service of the whole.' Palinor's response is typical of responses to such theodicies: 'No glass is dark enough to stand for the suffering of a tortured and dying child' (pp. 176–7).

On the other hand there are what one might call 'secret plan' defences that, instead of proposing a large-scale and general description of how evil is connected to a 'greater good', suggest that God allows each specific evil as a particular inscrutable step of his unimaginably complex plan, the end point of which is the great good of salvation. So the eleventh-century theologian Abelard says:

> Who could be unaware that God's highest goodness, which permits nothing to happen without a cause, arranges even evil things so well, and also uses them in the best way, so that it is true that it is good that these evil things happen, although the evil itself is in no way good?
>
> *Collationes*, II.210

Abelard's prime example is the evil of Judas' betrayal of Jesus: an evil act, which caused great harm – but which God arranged for good.

I have run through these descriptions quite quickly, and have not paused to unpack any of the nuances or complexities that their defenders and critics have explored. This is simply a sketch of what seems to me to be the 'standard conversation' about the problem of evil. It is a conversation that involves giving general answers to a general question: it does not rely upon detailed reference to the stories of particular evils (except as illustrative examples); it does not rely upon detailed reference to the Christian gospel. Faced with an argument that appears to disprove the existence of a good, omnipotent being by reference to the simple facts of evil's existence, persistence and prevalence, these defences show that the two sides of this abstract equation can in fact be reconciled – answering the challenge in the same generalized terms in which it was posed. But is that enough?

Exercise

Which of these defences, if any, do you find most convincing?

Notes

1 David Hume, *Dialogues Concerning Natural Religion*, ed. Norman Kemp Smith, London: Nelson, 1947, Pt. x, p. 198 (available online at <http://www.gutenberg.org/etext/4583>); he is paraphrasing an argument of Epicurus, cited in Lactantius, *De Ira Dei* XIII, available online at <http://www.ccel.org/ccel/schaff/anf07.html>

2 This is the '*logical* problem of evil' (for which the existence of evil contradicts the existence of a good God), as opposed to the '*evidential* problem of evil' for which the quantity, prevalence and persistence of evil constitutes evidence that the existence of a good God is improbable. I have taken my formulation of the logical problem from Christopher Southgate and Andrew Robinson, 'Varieties of Theodicy: An Exploration of Responses to the Problem of Evil Based on a Typology of Good–Harm Analyses' in Robert J. Russell, Nancey Murphy and William Stoeger (eds), *Physics and Cosmology: Scientific Perspectives on the Problem of Evil in Nature*, Berkeley, CA and Vatican City: CTNS and Vatican Observatory, 2006.

3 The phrase is from John Keats, 'Letter to George and Georgiana Keats, 21 April 1819' in H. E. Rollins (ed.), *Letters of John Keats 1814–1821*, Cambridge: Cambridge University Press, 1958, vol. 2.

3

Changing the Subject

This 'standard conversation' – the whole tradition of 'greater good' theodicy, working at a fairly general level – has come in for a good deal of serious criticism. Sometimes the criticisms have come from people who want to reform and improve the defences, and tie them a little more closely to the resources of the Christian gospel and to the details of actual evils. Sometimes, and particularly in recent years, the criticisms have come from people who reject the whole project of 'theodicy'.

This booklet is not long enough for us to spend time exploring all the relevant arguments, and making an informed judgement about whether the standard conversation has received a knock-out blow from its opponents, or whether it can be rescued by one means or another. For that, you can look at the References and Further Reading section. What I do hope to be able to do in the space available, however, is to indicate the *kind* of criticisms that have been levelled, and suggest how they might lead us to 'change the subject' – to rethink what the problem of evil is, and what kind of response it calls for.

Theodicy as anaesthetic?

The first criticism focuses on the fact that standard theodicies appear, implicitly or explicitly, to be aimed at allowing believers in God to *come to terms* with evil: to find a proper place for it in their thinking. Is it possible that one effect of such theodicy is to *anaesthetize* us to evil? Do such theodicies whisper in our ear, whenever we are faced with some situation of great suffering, 'It isn't as bad as all that; don't worry – it's quite proper that this sort of thing should happen, and in any case God will make it up to the victims in the end'? Might theodicy, by reconciling the existence of a good God with the existence of evil, reconcile *us* to evil?

Even if the logic of the theodicists' arguments is flawless, if those arguments lead us to make our peace with evil, then they are themselves evil. To construct a theodicy would, in this case, be like standing idly beside a stream in which someone is drowning, spending the last seconds of the drowner's life working out how you can live with the tragedy and still keep your faith.

When we turn on the television to see a news report of a young girl kidnapped and subjected to hours of horrendous torture and repeated rape before being killed and dumped in a ditch, is there not something disturbing about the attempt to see how this event might be a piece in a beautiful jigsaw – or about any attempt to 'make sense' of this that might lessen our revulsion and outrage, our sense that this event does not belong, that it stands as an offence against all goodness, and that it *should not be*?

The thinking and arguing that we do on this as on any other topic are not isolated activities taking place in some abstract mental sphere: they are the activities of men and women living life in the world, and it is as necessary to take responsibility for the effects of this activity as it is to take responsibility for the way we drive our cars or relate to our neighbours or invest our money or speak to our relatives. If theodicy blinds us to the evil of evil, we should not indulge in it.

Who, in any case, is theodicy for? This criticism suggests that it speaks primarily to *spectators*, not to victims, and not to those who share a world with victims and are bound to them by ties of love and responsibility. If we are to 'change the subject', then, it will have to be in the direction of some conversation about the problem of evil that treats us as *participants* – and that doesn't make it easier for us to bear the torments of others.

Exercise

What do you think?
Is theodicy an anaesthetic?

Letting God off the hook

The second criticism is related, in that it too suggests that theodicy brushes the true burden of suffering under the carpet. But rather than asking what this might do to *us*, the second criticism focuses on what it says about *God*.

The easiest way in to this criticism is to turn away from the abstract fact of evil and focus on particular evils. Think, for instance, about the painful death of Darwin's daughter Annie, or of that girl who was raped, tortured and murdered. Does it make moral sense to say that the sufferings of either of them were *justified* because of some 'greater good'? That is, can we look at the suffering and death of either as a 'price worth paying' in order to secure the existence of a greater good – say, the existence of beings capable of responding in loving freedom to God?

Almost everyone who discusses this question mentions at this point Fyodor Dostoevsky's *The Brothers Karamazov*, in which Ivan Karamazov makes an impassioned protest against the idea that any good future could be worth the price of one abused child's suffering. Ivan tells the story of a five-year-old child who had been tortured by her parents.

> They beat her, thrashed her, kicked her for no reason till her body was one bruise. Then, they went to greater refinements of cruelty – shut her up all night in the cold and frost in a privy, and … smeared her face and filled her mouth with excrement, and it was her mother, her mother did this. And that mother could sleep, hearing the poor child's groans! Can you understand why a little creature, who can't even understand what's done to her, should beat her little aching heart with her tiny fist in the dark and the cold, and weep her meek unresentful tears to dear, kind God to protect her?

For what greater good, Ivan asks, could this possibly be a price worth paying? What greater good is

> worth the tears of that one tortured child … If the sufferings of children go to swell the sum of sufferings which was necessary to pay for truth, then I protest that the truth is not worth such a price … [T]oo

high a price is asked for harmony; it's beyond our means to pay so much to enter on it. And so I hasten to give back my entrance ticket, and if I am an honest man I am bound to give it back as soon as possible. And that I am doing. It's not God that I don't accept, Alyosha, only I most respectfully return him the ticket. (ch. 35)

Exercise

Is Ivan Karamazov right?

Perhaps Ivan should not 'accept' this God, however. Surely any version of 'greater good' theodicy that simply involves God writing off Annie Darwin, or the raped and murdered girl, or the tortured child in the outhouse, in order to secure some greater good, has ceased to speak about a God worthy of worship?

What, however, if the greater good secured is not one that involves writing off the dead child? What if the greater good is one in which those children themselves will be tended and healed after death – so that it is not a matter of them being sacrificed to the greater good of others? Well, there are some conceptual difficulties about saying so that we would need to explore if we were treating this topic in more detail. For instance, if the dead child can be taken to a 'better place' without in the end having been robbed of anything irreplaceable, why couldn't she have been taken there in the first place? Why couldn't we all? What happens to the idea that this world of suffering is *necessary* to the good which God has for us if it is possible to be hoisted out of this world and taken straight to that good? But even if we ignore such questions, and accept that this consolation or healing is possible, and will constitute a greater good *for the suffering child herself*, that good stored up in the future does not make the present evil any less evil. The path that God has chosen, in this picture of things, is a path along which real evil happens, even if it is evil that is followed by consolation or healing.

One might compare what happens when a human being is faced with a choice between two evils, and can at best choose the lesser. The lesser of two evils is still evil, and while she might be justified, in the sense that no one could properly condemn her, she does not remain *innocent*: she can't avoid becoming the person who has done this evil thing, even if she could not have done anything different. Similarly, if we imagine God choosing this path that leads through evil to greater good, we are still imagining God choosing a path that leads through evil. Even if done for the sake of good, evil is still evil.

Suppose that I were faced, like Charles Darwin, with the prolonged and painful death of my own daughter. Whatever thoughts I might have about the consolation that God will have for her in future can and should do nothing to prevent what is happening now from being horrifying, from crushing my heart. Even if I were to grant everything to the theodicists' arguments, and agree that nothing about this terrible situation can tell me that God is not good, that would not prevent the situation being terrible; it would not prevent it being an abomination – something to which I can only properly react with horror. The philosopher D.Z. Phillips, drawing on a larger scale example, puts it this way:

> [W]hen evil is necessitated in terrible circumstances, the evil in the means is as objective as the good in what has to be done … If God can allow [the Holocaust] *without a second thought*, then, like Dostoevsky's Ivan Karamazov, we respectfully return him the ticket. If he allows it *after a second thought* [i.e., giving full weight to the objectivity of the evil, and taking responsibility for it], God is involved in sorrows in such a way that he cannot emerge morally unscathed. (Phillips, 2004, p. 46)

If we imagine a God who deliberately chooses the way of evil for the sake of a greater good, then we might, perhaps, be able to hold on to a belief in a good God, but it will now be a God who has reluctantly been forced to do evil, a God who has in one sense lost his innocence.

Neither I nor D.Z. Phillips is saying that this *is* the proper way to think about God's relation to the evil that happens. It is simply that this God who has lost his innocence is all that seems to be on offer at the end of a standard 'greater good' theodicy. We might, with that approach, get to the point where we can get God off the hook, and show that God could not have done otherwise. But we will still be left with a God who is, however unavoidably, involved in evil – who has been forced to *do* evil. If we are to 'change the subject', it will have to be in the direction of some conversation about the problem of evil that does not focus on getting God off the hook or demonstrating God's freedom from blame, but rather asks what God's goodness means if it has to do with God's passionate care for and loving involvement in every aspect of the world that God has made, however dark.

Is this the God of Jesus Christ?

This brings us to the threshold of the third main criticism of the standard conversation about theodicy. What God does this theodicy speak about? It speaks about a God who is good – and we have just seen that the kind of goodness it talks about might be suspect. But it also talks about a God who is powerful, indeed who is all-powerful, omnipotent. And it is perhaps here that the standard conversation most obviously fails, in that it describes a kind of power that has nothing to do with the God of the Christian gospel.

You will find a discussion of omnipotence in many of the texts in which the standard conversation about the problem of evil is carried on. They analyse God's nature as all-powerful, often in amazingly abstract terms. God, we are told, must have the power to do anything that is not logically contradictory; God is a being of absolutely unfettered freedom, who may do whatever God chooses.

This is not the God of the Christian gospel, because the understanding of power involved is one that is rejected by the gospel. The power of God that the gospel teaches us about is the power of love, and only the power of love. It is not that God is power, and has chosen love, but that God is love – and any power that God has is and can only be the power of that love. We can't talk about what God can and cannot do by considering in the abstract what 'omnipotent' must mean, but can only talk about what God can and cannot do by asking what the love revealed in the gospel can and cannot do. And while, yes, we will not be being faithful to Christian understanding of God's power unless we say that it is not constrained by anything that is *not* God, we must still say that God *is* constrained by who God is, and that God is love.

What power does God have? It is that power that is called weakness and foolishness in 1 Corinthians 1.25. More precisely, it is the power to become incarnate, and the power to die. That is, it is the power that we see clearly in Jesus of Nazareth, and most clearly on the cross – which is where, as John's Gospel tells us, God's glory is most visible. And, yes, Christianity has traditionally claimed that this power of divine love is at work in everything that happens, that it is the power that sustains, accompanies and guides the whole of creation in every moment of its existence, that it is invincible and indestructible, ever present and ever trustworthy – but it is all those things only as the power of love.

The standard conversation sometimes seems to miss this completely. D.Z. Phillips says of one of the proponents of the standard conversation that his arguments

> suggest that God's essential nature is sheer power, but that, now and again, at rather crucial moments, he decides not to exercise it. ... [T]he 'humbling' [i.e., the incarnation] seems to be a decision to do what he would not normally do. Orthodox Christian teaching, however, teaches that the 'humbling' teaches us something essential about God. That he took 'the form of a servant' is not meant to imply that normally his form is quite different. ... Rather, it implies that if God wanted to reveal something essential about himself on earth, 'the form of a servant' was itself essential to doing so. (Phillips, 2004, pp. 178–9)

If we are to 'change the subject', then, it will have to be in the direction of some conversation about the problem of evil that speaks about how a God with *this* kind of power relates to the evil in the world.

Exercise

Can you think of any ways in which we continue to claim for God, or expect from God, forms of power that are unrelated to love?

Do we know what we're talking about?

There is one more criticism that I want to explore. It is levelled against the implicit picture painted in the standard conversation of God choosing what kind of world to create by weighing up the costs and benefits. The criticism arises because it is not at all clear that we actually know what we're talking about if we talk about God like that. It is a way of talking about God that has lost its moorings in faith, and become idle and abstract speculation about God's means and methods.

I'm not trying to rule out all talk about the nature of God's creation of the world. The claim that the world we live in depends entirely upon God's loving will is properly a central one in Christian faith – as is the claim that this world rests *only* upon that loving will. Christians have expressed that latter claim by saying that God was not in any way *constrained* to create by something external to God.

I can also see the importance of saying that the divine will that underlies the world cannot be thought of as a selfish will. It is not to be thought of as the will of one who stands to gain something from creation, and so it is appropriate to express this by saying that God was not constrained to create *even by God's own nature.*

If we consider these deep-seated claims about the world's relationship to the love of God, we will be able to see the soil in which Christian talk about God's 'free decision' to create the world is rooted. The image of God freely choosing is a graphic way of trying to grasp and express these deep convictions that Christians have about the divine will that sustains and guides them, and that they trust sustains and guides all things. But this remains a way of trying to capture in a graspable image a reality that is, ultimately, ungraspable. We must acknowledge the inadequacy of words like freedom and constraint, internal and external, selfishness and love, decision and action, when we are speaking about the unfathomable reality of God's life. This image is given what content and mooring it has because it is rooted in the ways Christians have been taught by the gospel to see themselves and their world as faithfully and lovingly addressed and held by the God who is beyond their words. But, even though this image may be our best way of capturing this aspect of the Christian vision, it doesn't amount to a clear explanatory theory that tells us that God is not really so ungraspable, but is in fact something more or less like a human agent, and that creation was in fact something more or less like a human action, consequent upon something more or less like a human decision.

To think that we can speak meaningfully of the 'options' available to God, to think that we can speak of God engaged in a process of 'choosing', and to think that we can talk about this process involving God's 'weighing up' of prices that God is or is not willing to pay: that seems to me to assume that we do have just such a clear explanatory theory. It is to pull the language of God's creative freedom from its moorings and leave it bobbing about in our minds with nothing to hold on to.

It's not that I think we can say *nothing* about God's creation of this world, and so God's creation of a world in which there is evil. It's simply that I don't think we can say enough to launch a theodicy. Suppose we run with the ideas about God's power that I sketched at the end of the last section, for instance. We could quite appropriately say that the God known in Jesus Christ can't be thought to have the power to create a world over which he would rule as a despot – not because there is some external constraint preventing him from doing so, but because it makes no sense to say that *the God known in Jesus Christ* would do this. And we could similarly say that the only kind of creation that can be attributed to the Christian God is creation as an act of selflessness – which we might *picture* as God desiring not to be all that there is, God making space for an 'other' who is not simply an extension of God's own desires, God making something that is given its own way of being. 'Desiring', 'selflessness', 'making space' – all these are, of course, words that we know to be inadequate to the reality of God, and we know that we can't begin to imagine the reality to which they point. Yet these claims are given some content and mooring because they are rooted in the ways Christians have been taught by the gospel to see themselves and their world as addressed and held by God. These claims are given *just enough* content and mooring for us to go on speaking like this, and to know that our words are not simply empty. God's creative work is like this – in some respects. It resembles this – in part. Those resemblances, however, stand within a much greater dissimilarity: God is *not* more or less the same as a very powerful human being.

So on the one hand it does seem to make deep sense to speak of the Christian God creating a world that has its own integrity, structure and continuity – which has its own way of being that God upholds. It *is* deeply appropriate to speak of God giving time and space to creatures who can act not as the puppets of God's whims, but according to the structure, the nature, that God has given them – and who are, in that sense, made for freedom. And we might even say, when we see that the world's freedom and ours gives rise to evil, that *we* can't imagine how that could have been wholly avoided in our kind of free world.

On the other hand, I don't think that we have anywhere to stand if we try to turn all that into an *explanation* of the origin of the world, or of the evil in it, declaring that from what we know of the choices available, God 'had' to choose this one.

If we are to 'change the subject', then, it will have to be in the direction of some conversation about the problem of evil that tries to do justice to the ways in which our language about God is learned, and the faith in which it is anchored. And it will also have to be in the direction of some conversation about evil that does not rely too much upon our ability to explain *why* God had to make this kind of world.

4

A Different Approach

God is not any kind of object that we can scrutinize and explain. You can't have a theory of God, or an explanation of God. All our words fail us and our imaginations falter if we try to pin God down, not because we are not clever enough but because we are *creatures* and our words and imaginations are only fitted for grasping hold of creaturely realities. The Creator who is our source, sustainer and goal is beyond our understanding.

You could think of trying to understand God as like trying to see the sun. If you turn to look directly at the sun, you are blinded and see nothing. But you *can* see the world around you basking in the sun's light, and you can feel its warmth on your own skin. Similarly, God has made Godself known by loving us, and by making that love real for us in our lives; to learn to know God is to learn to know yourself and the world as having God's love pouring down upon you. To know God is to learn to recognize yourself and the world as loved, and as called to love.

You could also think of trying to know God as like trying to know a melody. God is like a melody playing eternally, and to know this melody is to hear it, and then to learn to play it for yourself – throwing yourself into it until it takes you over, until 'you are the music while the music lasts' (Eliot, 1944). That is, knowing God is not simply a matter of learning to see yourself and the world in a certain way – it is a matter of learning to *live* in a certain way, and of becoming in your own place and time a reflection of the love that God pours out upon you.

So, the heart of the question of theodicy is not, 'How do we construct a theory that explains how God can be loving and good, and still be the creator and sustainer of a world like this?' The question is rather,

'Can we see ourselves as loved, see the world around us as loved, and live in echoing response to that love, in such a world as this?' Can we go on saying 'God is love' in these ways in a world of suffering and destruction?

Of course, seeing yourself as loved, and seeing the world around you as loved, and living in echoing response to that love in the world, can't but involve you in *some* kind of thinking about and imagining of the One who is the source of this love, even if those thoughts and imaginings are attempts to picture the unpicturable, describe the indescribable, and so are bound to be inadequate to the ungraspable reality of God. But putting it this way round shows us that our ways of thinking about and imagining God are, in a sense, secondary: they rest upon, and draw life from, our recognition of and participation in the love that God pours out upon us. If I say, for instance, that 'God is omnipotent', I won't understand what that means by trying to come up with an abstract definition, and then arguing about what God must be able to do. I will discover what those words mean as I learn what it means to live with the trust that there is no situation in which God's love fails, no reality or extremity in which God's love is extinguished or finally defeated. And that's not something I'm going to understand in any depth by sitting here typing at my computer, or that you're going to understand in any depth by reading this booklet. It's not a matter of ideas and arguments, or definitions and defences: it's a matter of living, or of *learning* to live a certain way in the world. And it is tested not primarily by checking a set of arguments for validity, or a set of definitions for accuracy: it is tested by asking whether this way of living is possible in our world without delusion, escapism and insensitivity.

If we are to speak truly about God, then, and to speak truly about God's relationship to evil, the only way we can get going is by resisting the temptation to speak about God in the abstract, and instead to attend to the ways in which we are met by God's love, called by God to love, and enabled to live the love of God in our lives.

> ### Exercise
>
> What role do you think that 'arguments, definitions and defences' can and should play in sustaining Christian life? (And remember: that includes booklets like this, and discussions like the one you are having!)

The God of the covenant

Can Christians see themselves and their world as loved by God, without turning a blind eye to the suffering and destruction that pervade the world? Well, Christian (and Jewish) talk about God's love is rooted in God's covenant with Israel. Talk of a God of loving-kindness is not a deduction made by early theologians, based upon the harmony that they see in the world around them; it is not an explanation for the world's order and habitability, proposed by philosophers or the ancient equivalent of scientists. Talk of God's loving-kindness is not originally the province of those who see the world around them as Paley did, as a harmonious whole unbroken by any discordant note.

Talk of the loving-kindness of God is first found on the lips of those who recognize that they have been caught up in a *covenant* with God in history. And it is very often the province of those who trust in this covenant and call upon God to honour it at times of disaster, and in exile. God's loving-kindness is spoken of most clearly when the integrity and continuity of Israel is threatened and disrupted; we could say that talk of God's loving-kindness *has its home* in such times and places: it is above all the language of those who trust that the covenant is still there, deeper than their present trials.

Among the most characteristic forms taken by talk of God's loving-kindness, therefore, we find *protest*: calls upon God to fulfil the covenant promises; calls upon God to demonstrate what the worshipper trusts is true – that slavery, disaster, exile and death cannot break God's covenant. Take Psalm 89, for instance, which opens 'I will sing of the Lord's great love for ever!' and runs on for 37 verses of high praise for this God who 'founded the world and all that is in it' (v. 11). Yet later in the same Psalm we find the questions: 'How long, O Lord? Will you hide yourself for ever … Lord, where is your steadfast love of old, which by your faithfulness you swore to David?' (vv. 46, 49).

If this is where we find language about God's loving-kindness, then there are three things we can say about the problem of evil and the project of theodicy.

1. It is simply wrongheaded to say that the existence of slavery, disaster, exile and death *contradicts* talk of God's loving-kindness. Language about God's loving-kindness does not emerge as a theory about God that might then be challenged by the arrival of suffering and disorder. It emerges as a call upon God in the midst of suffering and disorder; it is, from the beginning, part of a way of life that responds to evil, and lives in the midst of evil.
2. Equally, to think that talk of God's loving-kindness should somehow *reconcile* us to slavery, disaster, exile and death is just as wrongheaded. Talk of God's loving-kindness is in part an expression of distress and incomprehension in the face of evil. In fact, it *sharpens* the worshippers' recognition and hatred of evil: it gives them a backdrop against which to see evil as evil – to see it as an intrusion, an abomination, something that should not be.
3. And, finally, talk of God's loving-kindness has nothing to do with letting God off the hook, or helping God to wash his hands of responsibility. Characteristically, talk of God's loving-kindness is an element in expressions of yearning and sometimes angry calls upon God in the midst of trials. God's people protest to him in the name of his own promises, not because they think God answerable to *them*, but because they think God answerable to God's own character: God's own promises are their court of appeal.

Exercise

How do protest and yearning find expression in our worship of God today?
Are they still strong notes in what we pray and sing?

The God of Jesus Christ

Christian talk about God is rooted even more deeply in what God has done for us in Jesus of Nazareth. Saying 'God is love' is, again, not a way of proposing an abstract theory about God's nature. It is a form of words that has its home in lives shaped by the recognition that God has met us in the life, death and resurrection of Jesus of Nazareth, and spoken love to us there. The claim that 'God is love' has its home among those who are discovering how to live in a way that will affirm and proclaim that Jesus' love for us was not simply a passing, accidental moment in the world's history, but a word spoken for the salvation of that whole world.

Just as with the talk of God's covenantal loving-kindness, talk of God's love that has its roots in encounter with Jesus is not a theory about God concocted when things were going well, which might then be tested when things go badly. The source of language about the love of God is, for Christians, a story in which violence, torture and execution, the denial and attempted destruction of love, are centre stage – and, from the start, Christians have affirmed both that the world to which Jesus came is 'his own' (John 1.11) (that is, that he belongs there, and that what he shows us is the deep truth of this world) *and* that this world crucified him. Christian talk of God's love is, from the beginning, part of a way of responding to and living in the midst of evil.

Of course, the story of Jesus is also a story of redemption and of resurrection: of God refusing to allow evil to have the last word. To go on saying 'God is love' in the face of evil is to trust in this God of redemption and resurrection, trusting in the power of love that worked in and through Jesus, rather than in some more abstract omnipotence or benevolence. But that means that the power in which Christians trust, the power to which they refer when they say 'God is love', is *not* the kind of power that steps in to prevent crucifixion. To trust in, or hope for, *that* kind of power is to trust in a different God from the one who is known here. The power in which Christians trust when they say 'God is love' is not a power that crashes in, all guns blazing, like the saviour in a Hollywood blockbuster. It is a power that works by 'weakness and foolishness': by becoming incarnate, and by dying.

It is also a power that works by resurrection. In the words of David Bentley Hart:

> As for comfort, when we seek it, I can imagine none greater than the happy knowledge that when I see the death of a child I do not see the face of God, but the face of His enemy. It is not a faith that would necessarily satisfy Ivan Karamazov, but neither is it one that his arguments can defeat: for it has set us free from optimism, and taught us hope instead. We can rejoice that we are saved not through the immanent mechanisms of history and nature, but by grace; that God will not unite all of history's many strands in one great synthesis, but will judge much of history false and damnable; that He will not simply reveal the sublime logic of fallen nature, but will strike off the fetters in which creation languishes; and that, rather than showing us how the tears of a small girl suffering in the dark were necessary for the building of the Kingdom, He will instead raise her up and wipe away all tears from her eyes – and there shall be no more death, nor sorrow, nor crying, nor any more pain, for the former things will have passed away, and He that sits upon the throne will say, 'Behold, I make all things new.' (Bentley Hart, 2003)

And in the words of Rowan Williams:

> If theologians speak at this point of the significance of post-mortem existence, it is not to justify or explain suffering, but to try and imagine a context ample enough for the subject of profound injury to grow into a different kind of self-perception. Such contexts exist in our ordinary experience, in therapeutic relationships, new kinds of communal life, and the sheer unpredictable range of stimulus that might or might not effect a transformation. For those whose death cuts them off from any such possibilities, theology can only point to its fundamental belief in a God who is faithful and eternal, and say, 'if there is hope, it lies there'. If it knows its business, it will not want to go much further. (Williams, 2007, p. 263)

> ### Exercise
> Do you think there is a danger of escapism in this focus upon life after death?

The God of those who suffer

So, I have argued that saying 'God is love' or 'God is good' is not a way of proposing an explanatory theory that brings with it claims about the choices available to God when he created the world. Instead, they are statements whose natural home is in the midst of suffering: they are statements of faith in a God who still holds us tight, even when all around is dark.

The question of evil is, therefore, not 'Can we reconcile the claim that God is good with the claim that there is evil?' Rather, the question is, 'Is it really possible for people to go on trusting in the covenant promises of God, and living in response to those promises, in the face of extremities of suffering?' and 'Is it possible for them to do so without evasion and delusion?'

Those are not questions that can be asked in the abstract, or answered in a short booklet. They are questions that are asked and answered in the lives of those who face actual evils, and particularly those who are taken to the extremities of suffering. To hold fast to God in lament and worship in the face of evil, and to carry on living out godly love in defiance of evil: *that* is what it means to say 'God is love'; that is what it means to affirm the goodness of God in defiance of evil. And, in the end, *only* the lives of those who face the extremities of evil in the name of God, with the love of God, provide the kind of answer to the problem of evil appropriate to Christianity.

Of course, we need to be very careful about how we make any claim like this. For every person who has faced the extremities of suffering in the name of God, with the love of God, there are others whose faith and love have all too understandably been destroyed. I am not recommending that we tally up the scores; this is not about constructing arguments that will prove to sceptics that the Christian vision is true. And it is not (heaven forbid!) about saying that suffering is *justified* because in some cases it produces people who respond so nobly. And it is certainly not about saying that those whom suffering crushes are to be blamed, or silenced, or passed over quickly for the sake of our faith. If faith and love persist in the face of the extremities of suffering, Christians cannot think of it as an *achievement* – an heroic effort on the part of the sufferer. It is a *gift*, a gift of God's grace, which they and we can only receive with thankfulness.

I am, rather, claiming that the lives of those who face the extremities of suffering open-eyed, but with faith and love, show us something about the nature of our faith. They show us that faith in God's love does not *have* to be destroyed in the extremity of suffering, and does not *have* to be a form of delusion or evasion in such extremity – but that it can be a way of living with and responding to such suffering: a way of winning a kind of victory over such suffering, even while being crucified by it. They perhaps show those of us who have not been pushed to such extremity that we can hold to our own faith with integrity, without denying the existence of extreme suffering, or betraying those who do suffer such extremity. And those who suffer in this way become for us, like Christ in the passion, signs that teach us what faith and love mean when they are stripped of all consolations and comforts – and so signs that teach us what true faith and love are like everywhere. Such lives are the only theodicy worth having.

5

Conclusion

There are two huge gaps in this booklet – gaps which mean that, if you've understood it and if you agree with it, you'll put the booklet away with dissatisfaction and go out and do something more useful instead.

In the first place, there is the fact that, in the previous chapter, I told no actual stories, either of those who had faced the extremities of suffering in faith and love, or of those who had been crushed. I skipped from talking about the need to attend to such witnesses to talking about the implications once we have done so. I'm afraid I could not see a way in which, in the space available, I could include such stories without so squashing them down that they became glib anecdotes, devoid of all the texture and depth that would make them worthwhile – all the honesty and directness which would *show* you what happens to faith and love when they are squeezed of all easy consolations, and that would allow you with fear and trembling to ask whether what you read is a product of evasion and delusion, or of open-eyed realism.

Of course, you know where to look for one such story: you have four versions of it bound into your Bibles at the start of the New Testament. But if you want to pursue this further, you will need to fill the gap I've left, and look to and learn from those whose lives follow the pattern of Jesus' own, through their own Gethsemanes and Golgothas. I've made some initial suggestions in the reading list at the end – but it is not only in books that the witness of those who suffer can be found.

There is another gap, though. What I have just said could still sound as if you and I are spectators, looking to the witness of those who suffer so as to bolster and justify our faith: seeing their lives, fates and faith as proofs that our faith is secure. We are *not* spectators, however. We suffer ourselves, and we share the same world as all who suffer, and the question is not whether our faith is intellectually justifiable in such a world, but whether we can learn to respond to that world in a way consistent with the claim that God is love. The point is not to get to the end of this booklet and breathe a sigh of relief because a problem has been solved; this booklet contains no *answer* to the problem of evil. No argument responds adequately to evil, not even an argument properly supplemented with the stories of those who have suffered. The only response that means anything is found in lives shaped by protest, by lament, and by Christ-like love. If we do not have those things, then no theodicy will help us; if we do, then we are – however feebly, however falteringly – participants in the only answer that the problem of evil needs.

References

Abelard, *Collationes*, ed. John Marenbon and Giovanni Orlandi, Oxford: Clarendon, 2001, II.210, p. 211, translation modified

Charles Darwin, *The Foundations of the Origin of Species: Two Essays Written in 1842 and 1844*, ed. Francis Darwin, Cambridge: Cambridge University Press, 1909, available online at <http://darwin-online.org.uk/EditorialIntroductions/Freeman_Sketchesof1842and1844.html>

Fyodor Dostoevsky, *The Brothers Karamazov*

T. S. Eliot, 'The Dry Salvages', in *Four Quartets*, London: Faber, 1944, 3.V., lines 211–12

Marilyn McCord Adams, *Horrendous Evils and the Goodness of God*, Ithaca and London: Cornell University Press, 1999

William Paley, *The Works of William Paley*, vol. 4, *Natural Theology*, London: Davison, 1830

Jill Paton Walsh, *Knowledge of Angels*, London: Black Swan, 1994

Kenneth Surin, *Theology and the Problem of Evil*, Oxford: Blackwell, 1986

Alfred Lord Tennyson, *In Memoriam A.H.H.*, London: E. Moxon, 1850, §§LIII, LV, available online at < http://www.theotherpages.org/poems/books/tennyson/tennyson01.html>

Nick Trakakis, 'The Evidential Problem of Evil', *The Internet Encyclopedia of Philosophy*, <http://www.iep.utm.edu/e/evil-evi.htm>, accessed 17 November 2006

'Tsunami and Theodicy', *First Things* 151, March 2005, pp. 6–9, p. 6, available online at <http://www.firstthings.com/ftissues/ft0503/opinion/hart.html> – quoting Revelation 21

Voltaire, *Toleration and other Essays*, ed. Joseph McCabe, New York and London: G.P. Putnam's, 1912, pp. 255–63, available online at <http://oll.libertyfund.org/Texts/Voltaire0265/OnToleration/HTMLs/0029_Pt05_Lisbon.html>

Rowan Williams, 'Redeeming Sorrows: Marilyn McCord Adams and the Defeat of Evil' in *Wrestling with Angels: Conversations in Modern Theology*, London: SCM, 2007

Further Reading

The standard conversion

James R. Beebe, 'The Logical Problem of Evil', in *The Internet Encyclopedia of Philosophy*, <http://www.iep.utm.edu/e/evil-log.htm>
John Hick, *Evil and the God of Love*, London: Macmillan, 1966
Alvin Plantinga, *God, Freedom, and Evil*, Grand Rapids, MI: Eerdmans, 1977
Richard Swinburne, *Providence and the Problem of Evil*, Oxford: Clarendon, 1998
Michael Tooley, 'The Problem of Evil' in *The Stanford Encyclopedia of Philosophy*, <http://plato.stanford.edu/entries/evil/>, 2002

Challenges to the standard conversion

Marilyn McCord Adams, *Horrendous Evils and the Goodness of God*, Ithaca and London: Cornell University Press, 1999
Karen Kilby, 'Evil and the Limits of Theology', The Centre of Theology and Philosophy, 2003, <http://theologyphilosophycentre.co.uk/papers/Kilby_EvilandLimits.doc>
D. Z. Phillips, *The Problem of Evil and the Problem of God*, London: SCM, 2004
Kenneth Surin, *Theology and the Problem of Evil*, Oxford: Blackwell, 1986
Terrence W. Tilley, *The Evils of Theodicy*, Washington, DC: Georgetown University Press, 1991

Ways forward

David Bentley Hart, *The Doors of the Sea: Where was God in the Tsunami?*, Grand Rapids: Eerdmans, 2005
Stanley Hauerwas, *Naming the Silences: God, Medicine and the Problem of Suffering*, Edinburgh: T&T Clark, 1993
Margaret Spufford, *Celebration*, London: Fount, 1989
Margaret Spufford, 'A Revelation of Divine Love' in Ann Loades, *Spiritual Classics from the Late Twentieth Century*, London: The National Society / Church House Publishing, 1995
Elie Wiesel, *Night*, London: MacGibbon and Key, 1960
N. T. Wright, *Evil and the Justice of God*, London: SPCK, 2006